Y13

EXPLORING COUNTRIES

Argentina

by Kari Schuetz

BELLWETHER MEDIA • MINNEAPOLIS, MN

BLASTOFF!
5
READERS

Note to Librarians, Teachers, and Parents:

Blastoff! Readers are carefully developed by literacy experts and combine standards-based content with developmentally appropriate text.

Level 1 provides the most support through repetition of high-frequency words, light text, predictable sentence patterns, and strong visual support.

Level 2 offers early readers a bit more challenge through varied simple sentences, increased text load, and less repetition of high-frequency words.

Level 3 advances early-fluent readers toward fluency through increased text and concept load, less reliance on visuals, longer sentences, and more literary language.

Level 4 builds reading stamina by providing more text per page, increased use of punctuation, greater variation in sentence patterns, and increasingly challenging vocabulary.

Level 5 encourages children to move from "learning to read" to "reading to learn" by providing even more text, varied writing styles, and less familiar topics.

Whichever book is right for your reader, Blastoff! Readers are the perfect books to build confidence and encourage a love of reading that will last a lifetime!

This edition first published in 2012 by Bellwether Media, Inc.

No part of this publication may be reproduced in whole or in part without written permission of the publisher. For information regarding permission, write to Bellwether Media, Inc., Attention: Permissions Department, 5357 Penn Avenue South, Minneapolis, MN 55419.

Library of Congress Cataloging-in-Publication Data

Schuetz, Kari.
 Argentina / by Kari Schuetz.
    p. cm. – (Exploring countries) (Blastoff! readers)
 Summary: "Developed by literacy experts for students in grades three through seven, this book introduces young readers to the geography and culture of Argentina"–Provided by publisher.
 Includes bibliographical references and index.
 ISBN 978-1-60014-616-9 (hardcover : alk. paper)
 1. Argentina–Juvenile literature. I. Title.
 F2808.2.S38 2012
 982–dc22
                                    2011002225

Printed in the United States of America, North Mankato, MN.

080111   1187

Contents

Brazil

Bolivia

Paraguay

Chile

Uruguay

Buenos Aires

Argentina

Did you know?

Argentina comes from the Latin word argentum, which means "silver." European explorers believed Argentina's land was rich with this precious metal.

Strait
of
Magellan

Falkland
Islands

**Atlantic
Ocean**

Argentina is the second-largest
country in South America.
It spans 1,073,518 square miles
(2,780,400 square kilometers)
between the Andes Mountains
and the Atlantic Ocean. It is
bordered by Uruguay, Brazil,
Paraguay, Bolivia, and Chile.
Buenos Aires, Argentina's capital,
is located close to Uruguay.

Argentina is divided into
23 **provinces**. The **Strait** of
Magellan separates the southern
province of Tierra del Fuego from the
rest of the country. Argentina claims
the Falkland Islands, South Georgia,
the South Sandwich Islands, and a
part of Antarctica as its **territories**.

Andes Mountains

Argentina's landscape has great **diversity**. The Andes Mountains run along the country's western border. This range includes Mount Aconcagua, the highest peak in the **Western Hemisphere**. This mountain rises 22,831 feet (6,959 meters) above sea level.

Lowlands stretch across most of northern Argentina. The flat area between the Andes and the Paraná River is called Gran Chaco. Grasslands called the Pampas fill central Argentina. These plains are dry in the east and damp in the west. **Glaciers** dot Patagonia, the country's southern **plateau**.

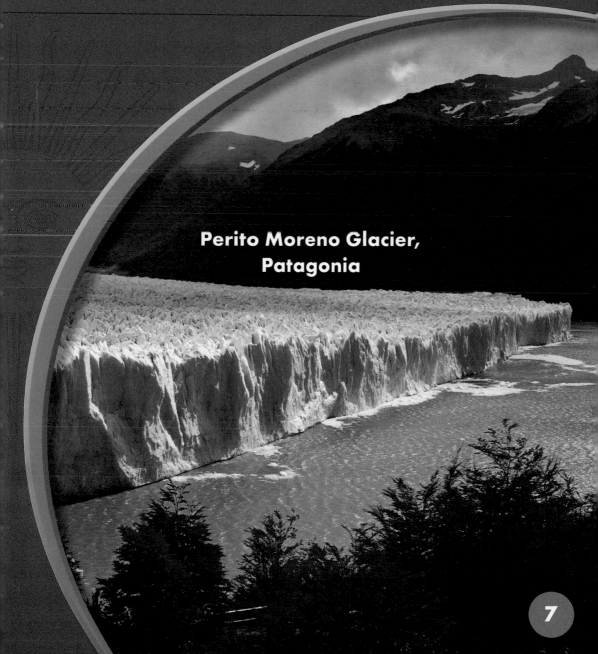

Perito Moreno Glacier, Patagonia

Argentina is known for its beautiful waterfalls. Iguazú Falls, which runs between Argentina and Brazil, is the country's most popular group of waterfalls. It divides the Iguazú River in two. The falls formed about 100 million years ago.

Iguazú comes from the language of South America's Guaraní people. The word means "great water."

Rocky islands within the falls create 275 separate waterfalls. The most famous one is called the Devil's Throat. It is the shape of a horseshoe and plunges 269 feet (82 meters). Giant rainbows often appear in its mist.

guanacos

Many different animals live in Argentina. Jaguars, puma, and ocelots stalk capybaras and tapirs in the country's **lush** forests. Several kinds of poisonous snakes, including yararacas, slither there in search of prey. Pudús, the smallest deer in the world, live in the Andes Mountains near Patagonia. Guanacos also roam these highlands.

Did you know?

Plains viscachas scurry across the Pampas of Argentina. These rodents look like rabbits with mustaches!

plains viscacha

Andean condor

three-banded armadillo

fun fact

Three-banded armadillos live in the Gran Chaco region of Argentina. They can roll up into a ball to escape danger!

A variety of birds live throughout Argentina's landscape. Near the country's southern tip, penguins swim in the **frigid** waters. Toucans and hummingbirds fly in warmer, tropical areas. Flightless birds called rheas make their homes in many **habitats**. The world's largest vulture, the Andean condor, soars above the mountains. This bird has a wingspan of 10 feet (3 meters)!

Did you know?

European explorers first came to the lands of Argentina in 1516. Argentina was part of a Spanish colony founded in 1580.

More than 41.5 million people live in Argentina. Almost all Argentines have **ancestors** who were **immigrants** from countries in Europe. Most have Spanish or Italian roots. Now, people from the Middle East and Asia also live in the country.

Native peoples, including the Guarani, are scattered across Argentina in small numbers. *Mestizos* make up a small part of Argentina's population. These are people with both European and native backgrounds. Most Argentines speak Spanish, which is the country's official language.

Speak Spanish!

English	Spanish	How to say it
hello	hola	OH-lah
good-bye	adios	ah-dee-OHS
yes	sí	SEE
no	no	NOH
please	por favor	POHR fah-VOR
thank you	gracias	GRAH-see-uhs
friend (male)	amigo	ah-MEE-goh
friend (female)	amiga	ah-MEE-gah

Daily Life

Most Argentines make their homes in or near large cities. They live in high-rise apartments or single-story homes. To get around, they take taxis or ride city buses called *colectivos*. They often shop and stroll in city plazas.

14

Only about 1 out of every 10 Argentines lives in the countryside. They live in small houses or on farms. People in the countryside often travel to nearby cities to find work and buy goods.

countryside
8%

cities
92%

15

The school year in Argentina begins in March and ends in December. Most children between the ages of 3 and 5 attend preschools across the country. Children begin primary school when they are 6 years old. They must attend for six or seven grades, depending on the school. Students study math, social studies, science, and Spanish. They also take classes in physical education, music, and art. After primary school, they can attend several years of secondary school. This prepares them for a **vocational school** or a university.

Did you know?

Teachers in Argentina use numbers instead of letters to grade their students. The worst grade is 1 and the best is 10.

17

Where People Work
in Argentina

manufacturing 23%

services 72%

farming 5%

Most Argentines have **service jobs** in cities. Many work in stores, hotels, and restaurants. Some drive taxis or buses. Factory workers make food products and cars that are shipped to countries around the world.

In the countryside, Argentines work the land. Farmers grow wheat, corn, soybeans, and fruits in the Pampas and to the north. Some raise cattle, hogs, and sheep. Throughout the country, people drill for oil and natural gas. They dig into the earth for **minerals** such as iron ore and copper. Along the coasts, fishermen catch squids, shrimp, and many kinds of fish.

pato

People in Argentina enjoy many sports. Soccer is the most popular sport across the country. Many Argentines play in leagues and watch their national team compete in the **World Cup**. *Pato* is Argentina's national sport. Players ride horses and try to throw a ball into the other team's goal.

Argentines enjoy many other activities. Some ski down the slopes of the Andes Mountains. Others move to the beat of the Argentine *tango*. Many Argentines go see movies or watch dramas and game shows on television.

Argentine *tango*

asado

fun fact

Argentines often eat late in the evening. Many sit down for dinner after 9 PM.

Argentines eat a lot of meat, especially beef. Cooks prepare *asado*, or barbequed beef, over an open fire or on a grill called a *parrilla*. Meat pies known as *empanadas* are also a common meal.

A popular drink across Argentina is *maté*. It is made from the leaves of the *yerba maté* plant. A special straw called a *bombilla* is often used to sip this drink from a gourd. Argentines love to eat desserts and sweets. Ice cream, or *helado*, is enjoyed throughout the country. Many people eat cakes and pastries topped with *dulce de leche*, a kind of caramel.

empanada

maté

dulce de leche **cake**

! fun fact

During *Carnival*, Argentines build huge floats that parade down the street with dancers and musicians.

Independence Day

Most people in Argentina are Christians. They celebrate Christmas, Easter, and other Christian holidays. Two weeks before the Christian season of **Lent**, many Argentines celebrate *Carnival*. During this holiday, dancers, singers, and musicians entertain huge crowds.

Argentina's national holidays include First Patriotic Government Day and Independence Day. On May 25, Argentines remember the May Revolution of 1810 as they celebrate First Patriotic Government Day. They watch parades and listen to the country's national anthem. Independence Day takes place on July 9. It marks the day in 1816 when Argentina declared its freedom from Spain.

South American cowboys, or *gauchos*, roamed the Pampas of Argentina in the 1700s and 1800s. They were **nomads** who chased the wild cattle that wandered the plains. They wore pants called *bombachas* and traditional *ponchos*. Many of them owned nothing but a horse and a few tools.

Gauchos carried several important tools. These included a knife, a leather whip, and a throwing rope known as a *bola*. Their tools helped them live freely off the land. Today, *gauchos* are a symbol of Argentina to people around the world. They represent the spirit, landscape, and independence of Argentina.

Fast Facts About Argentina

Argentina's Flag

The flag of Argentina has three horizontal stripes. The top and bottom stripes are light blue, and the middle stripe is white. The colors stand for clear skies and the snow-covered Andes Mountains. A golden sun sits in the center of the flag. It represents the day of the May Revolution of 1810 when the sun shone through the clouds. Argentina's current flag was adopted on February 25, 1818.

Official Name: Argentine Republic

Area: 1,073,518 square miles
                          (2,780,400 square kilometers);
                          Argentina is the 8th largest
                          country in the world.

Capital City:	Buenos Aires
Important Cities:	Córdoba, La Plata
Population:	41,769,726 (July 2011)
Official Language:	Spanish
National Holidays:	First Patriotic Government Day (May 25), Independence Day (July 9)
Religions:	Christian (94%), Other (6%)
Major Industries:	farming, fishing, forestry, manufacturing, mining, services
Natural Resources:	lead, zinc, tin, copper, iron ore, manganese, oil, uranium, silver, natural gas
Manufactured Products:	food products, cars, clothing, chemicals, metals
Farm Products:	soybeans, corn, wheat, fruits, sunflower seeds, vegetables, tea, peanuts, beef
Unit of Money:	Argentine peso; the peso is divided into 100 centavos.

Glossary

ancestors—relatives who lived long ago

diversity—variety; Argentina's landscape has a diversity of features.

frigid—extremely cold

glaciers—massive sheets of ice that cover a large area of land

habitats—environments in which plants or animals usually live

immigrants—people who leave one country to live in another country

Lent—the forty weekdays before the Christian holiday of Easter

lush—growing quickly and heavily

minerals—elements found in nature; iron ore and copper are examples of minerals.

native—originally from a specific place

nomads—people who move freely from place to place

plateau—an area of flat, raised land

provinces—areas within a country; provinces follow all the laws of the country and make some of their own laws.

service jobs—jobs that perform tasks for people or businesses

strait—a narrow stretch of water that connects two larger bodies of water

territories—areas of land that belong to a country; Argentina claims the Falkland Islands, South Georgia, the South Sandwich Islands, and a part of Antarctica as its territories.

vocational school—a school that trains students to do specific jobs

Western Hemisphere—the half of Earth west of the prime meridian; the Western Hemisphere includes North America and South America.

World Cup—an international soccer competition held every four years

To Learn More

AT THE LIBRARY

Lamm, C. Drew. *Gauchada*. New York, N.Y.:
Random House, 2001.

Pohl, Kathleen. *Looking at Argentina*. Pleasantville,
N.Y.: Gareth Stevens Pub., 2008.

Shields, Charles J. *Argentina*. Philadelphia, Pa.:
Mason Crest Publishers, 2009.

ON THE WEB

Learning more about Argentina
is as easy as 1, 2, 3.

1. Go to www.factsurfer.com.

2. Enter "Argentina" into the search box.

3. Click the "Surf" button and you will see a list of
   related Web sites.

With factsurfer.com, finding more information is just
a click away.

Index

The images in this book are reproduced through the courtesy of: Radius Images/Photolibrary, front cover, pp. 6, 8-9, Matias Raman, front cover (flag), p. 28; Juan Martinez, pp. 4, 5, 23 (middle); Pablo H Caridad, p. 7; Robert Seitz/Photolibrary, pp. 10-11; M&G Therin-Weise/Age Fotostock, p. 11 (top); H Schmidbauer/Age Fotostock, p. 11 (middle); Mark Payne Gill/naturepl.com, p. 11 (bottom); Gilles Barbier/Photolibrary, p. 12; Chad Ehlers/Photolibrary, p. 14; David R. Frazier Photolibrary, Inc./Alamy, p. 15; AFP/Getty Images, pp. 16-17; Yadid Levy/Photolibrary, p. 18; Mark Edwards/Photolibrary, p. 19 (left); Shelby Ross/Getty Images, p. 19 (right); Eduardo Marichio Rivero/Alamy, p. 20; Luis Padilla/Photolibrary, p. 21; Ron Giling/Photolibrary, p. 22; Daniel Korzeniewski, p. 23 (top); Analia Valeria Urani, p. 23 (bottom); Natacha Pisarenko/AP Images, p. 24; Danita Delimont/Alamy, p. 25; Jefferson Bernardes/Getty Images, pp. 26-27; Kobby Dagan, p. 27 (small); Angel Placios, p. 29.